Original title:
Arctic Lanterns

Copyright © 2024 Swan Charm
All rights reserved.

Author: Linda Leevike
ISBN HARDBACK: 978-9916-79-807-2
ISBN PAPERBACK: 978-9916-79-808-9
ISBN EBOOK: 978-9916-79-809-6

The Glow Beneath the Stars

In the quiet of night,
Dreams sparkle like diamonds,
Beneath the vast sky,
Whispers of wonder call.

The moon's soft embrace,
Casts shadows that dance,
Every twinkle a story,
Of love and lost time.

With each flickering light,
Hearts beat in rhythm,
The universe listens,
To secrets of souls.

Stars drip like honey,
On the canvas of night,
A tapestry woven,
Of wishes and hope.

Together we stand,
Under cosmic display,
The glow of our hearts,
Guided by starlight.

Winter's Luminescent Secrets

Snowflakes whisper softly,
As they kiss the ground,
Blanketing the earth,
In shimmering silence.

Frost adorns the trees,
With glimmers of ice,
Nature's quiet magic,
Hides warmth in its breath.

Candlelight glows bright,
In the chill of the night,
Echoes of laughter,
Dance through frosty air.

Moonlight paints shadows,
On a canvas so white,
Every corner gleams,
With winter's embrace.

Amidst the stillness,
Secrets softly flow,
Winter holds close,
Its luminescent heart.

Veils of Ice and Light

Crystal shards of winter,
Hang like jewels above,
Veils of ice glistening,
In the morning sun.

Each breath forms a cloud,
In the biting air,
Nature's artistry flows,
In stillness and grace.

The light breaks through trees,
In a radiant burst,
Illuminating paths,
Hidden in the frost.

A dance of shadows,
And sparkles collide,
Veils whisper secrets,
Of seasons and change.

Underneath it all,
Life waits for rebirth,
In veils of ice and light,
Hope glimmers anew.

Glittering Horizons in the North

The northern lights surge,
Across the dark canvas,
A ballet of colors,
That ignites the night sky.

Mountains stand in silence,
Their peaks kissed by gold,
As horizons shimmer,
With magic untold.

Each hour unfolds treasures,
In the heart of the chill,
As nature reveals,
Her enchanting will.

Stars twinkle like fireflies,
In a velvet sea,
Whispers of the ancients,
Guide the wanderer free.

In the glow of the dusk,
Hearts dance in delight,
Chasing horizons,
Where dreams take flight.

Snow-Mantled Secrets of the Night

Beneath the stars, the world turns white,
Whispers carried on the crisp night air.
Footsteps silent, shadows take flight,
A blanket of snow, a soothing layer.

Moonlight dances on the frozen ground,
Secrets nestled in the winter's embrace.
Each flake a story waiting, unbound,
In this stillness, time finds its place.

Branches bow low, heavy with frost,
Nature's hush, a moment to treasure.
Silent beauty found, never lost,
In snow-mantled dreams, we find our measure.

Glimmers of hope in the chill of night,
As breath forms clouds in the pale moon's glow.
A canvas painted, serene delight,
In winter's heart, where memories flow.

So tread lightly on this sacred ground,
Where secrets gather in the cold, pure light.
In snow-mantled whispers, truth is found,
Wrapped in the magic of the night.

Ethereal Reflections on Crystal Waters

Glistening droplets touch the shore,
Ripples dance under the soft sun's gaze.
Mirror-like stillness, a tranquil pour,
Where dreams float lightly in the day's haze.

Mountains embrace the water's edge,
Tranquility kissed by the azure hue.
Nature's art, a soft pledge,
Infinite moments within each view.

Birdsong echoes, a gentle tune,
As petals drift on the lapping tide.
Beneath the sun, beneath the moon,
Waves bring solace where spirits abide.

A canvas vibrant, alive with light,
Each ripple tells tales of old and new.
In crystal waters, hearts take flight,
Ethereal reflections guide us through.

Let sweet breezes carry your dreams,
As you wander along this shimmering path.
In the embrace of nature, it seems,
Life's gentle melody unfolds its math.

Serene Flickers in the Deep Blue

Beneath the surface, wonders thrive,
Glimmers caught in the depths below.
Colors bloom where creatures strive,
In the embrace of the sea's soft flow.

Coral gardens sway with grace,
Life dances to rhythms unseen.
Each flicker a hint of nature's face,
In watery realms, forever serene.

A world alive where silence speaks,
With secrets nestled in shadows deep.
In this sanctuary, the heart seeks,
In the stillness, there's promise to keep.

Gentle currents guide the way,
As mermaids whisper in azure glow.
Time slips softly, hour by day,
In the deep blue depths, our spirits flow.

So let your worries drift away,
Caught in dreams of the ocean's song.
In serene flickers, we shall play,
In the great blue vastness, we belong.

Celestial Flames in the Winter's Heart

Stars ignite in the crystal sky,
Whispers of warmth in the frosty air.
Celestial flames hum their lullaby,
In winter's heart, love finds its share.

Glistening embers in velvet night,
Illuminate paths where spirits roam.
Each spark a wish, a beacon bright,
Guiding lost souls back to their home.

Crackling fires set to the tune,
Of stories woven from dusk till dawn.
In the embrace of a midnight boon,
Hearts ignite where hope is reborn.

Through snow-kissed whispers, dreams unfold,
As passions dance in the winter's chill.
Celestial tales waiting to be told,
In the warmth of love, we find our will.

So gather 'round the flickering glow,
Let memories warm you through the night.
In celestial flames, we come to know,
Together we shine, a radiant light.

Illuminated Silence of the Glacier

Silent whispers fill the air,
Underneath the icy glare.
Gentle shadows softly fall,
Nature's hush, a sacred call.

Crystal peaks, in moonlight's grace,
Timeless beauty, still embrace.
Fragments dance in evening's glow,
Here, the heartache ceases flow.

Frozen rivers run so deep,
Secrets in the silence sleep.
Each breath feels like a dream,
Echoes calm as daylight's beam.

Nature's canvas, white and blue,
Every layer tells the true.
In the stillness, time stands still,
Glacier's pride, a kindred thrill.

The Luminous Dance of Winter

Softly falls the silver snow,
In the moonlight's gentle glow.
Frozen branches sway and swing,
Whispers of the frost they bring.

Dancing shadows, crisp and bright,
Winter's charm, a tranquil sight.
Each snowflake, unique and bold,
Tales of winter, softly told.

Underneath a cloak of white,
Stars awaken in the night.
Frosty breath in the still air,
Nature's beauty, pure and rare.

Crash of ice, a sweet refrain,
Echoes drift across the plain.
Among the pines, a quiet trance,
Winter's song, a solemn dance.

Glistening Dreams on Frigid Shores

Waves of ice kiss the sand,
Whispers drift across the land.
Glistening like diamonds bright,
Frigid shores, a wondrous sight.

The horizon meets the sky,
Where the frozen waters lie.
In the distance, echoes play,
Dreams unfurl by light of day.

Footprints left by spirits past,
Carried on the winter's blast.
In each ripple, tales revive,
In this place, the heart's alive.

Crystal fog hangs in the air,
Mysteries linger everywhere.
Beneath the calm, a song remains,
Woven deep within the grains.

Echoes of Light in a Snowbound Realm

In the woods, the silence sings,
Snowflakes dance on feathered wings.
Every branch a story old,
Whispers wrapped in crystal cold.

Luminous trails guide the way,
Through the frost, the sun's warm ray.
In this realm of softest white,
Hope ignites the winter night.

Glistening paths of frost and fire,
Feed the soul with pure desire.
As we wander, hearts align,
In the cold, the warmth we find.

Echoes of a golden hue,
Fill the air with dreams anew.
In this snowbound, sacred place,
Find the light, embrace the grace.

Ethereal Flames of the North

In whispered winds the spirits dance,
Flickers of warmth in a wintry trance.
Auroras weave the night sky's cloak,
Colors ignite where the silence spoke.

Beneath the stars, a tale unfolds,
Ancient fires in the cold, so bold.
Embers rise, casting shadows wild,
Nature's magic, forever beguiled.

The pines stand tall, a watchful guard,
As flames embrace the night, a bard.
Songs of the north in rhythms flow,
An ethereal dance, soft and slow.

In this realm of shimmering light,
The darkness fades, giving way to bright.
With every spark, dreams take their flight,
Under the gaze of the endless night.

Glow of the Icebound Nights

Crystals glitter on a frozen lake,
Whispers of stories the stillness makes.
Moonlight kisses the blanket of snow,
In the chill of night, secrets grow.

Silent echoes through the biting air,
A haunting melody of midnight prayer.
The world wrapped tight in a frosty sigh,
Where dreams drift softly, like clouds in the sky.

Gentle shadows play on the hills,
The sparkle of stars, the heart gently thrills.
Each breath is visible, a soft puff of white,
In the tender embrace of icebound nights.

Nature's canvas, a shimmering scene,
Where silence reigns, calm and serene.
In the glow of frost, life takes a chance,
A dance of the night, an ethereal glance.

Twinkling Spires Against the Dark

In the stillness, the spires rise,
Against the dark, they pierce the skies.
A silhouette in twilight's glow,
Guiding the lost with a gentle show.

Each twinkle sings of worlds unseen,
Where dreams are woven through the serene.
The night holds magic, a silent spark,
A promise placed in the quiet dark.

Beneath the dome of a starlit veil,
Hopes take flight, as whispers sail.
The spires stand firm, a beacon bright,
Guardians of wonder in the cloak of night.

As shadows linger, the heart takes heed,
These twinkling spires plant every seed.
In the tapestry of time's enduring art,
Against the dark, they play their part.

Gleaming Under the Northern Dome

In the cradle of night, a gleaming show,
Under the northern dome, where cold winds blow.
Stars shimmer bright, like diamonds afar,
Guiding the wanderers, each wish a star.

The world below in a tranquil state,
Nature's rhythm, a silent fate.
Frosted dreams in the air do linger,
The magic of night held by a gentle finger.

With every breath, the cosmos sings,
Wrapped in wonder, life takes wings.
As the heavens swirl in colors divine,
Glimmers of hope in a grand design.

Underneath this vast, enchanted dome,
Hearts find solace, and spirits roam.
In the gleam of the night, we're never alone,
For the northern lights call us home.

Glowing Spirits of the Tundra

In the quiet night, they gather bright,
Whispers of warmth, a shimmering light.
Dancing above in the starry dome,
Guiding the lost, they call them home.

Beneath the vast sky, the spirits soar,
Lighting the paths of legends and lore.
With colors that twist, they weave and spin,
A tapestry rich where dreams begin.

Through icy winds, their laughter resounds,
Echoes of joy in the frosty surrounds.
In silence, they flicker, in motion, they glide,
Emboldening hope, like a warm, gentle tide.

Each shimmering glow tells tales of old,
Of journeys embarked and brave hearts bold.
With each pulse, the stories ignite,
The glowing spirits bless the night.

In the tundra's embrace, they play and gleam,
A spectral dance, like a vivid dream.
Forever they'll twinkle, forever they'll shine,
Glowing spirits, in perfect design.

A Beacon in the Frozen Night

Amidst the icy silence, a flicker glows,
A steadfast flame where the cold wind blows.
Standing alone on the edge of the sea,
A beacon of hope, calling out to me.

Its warmth wraps around like a soft, warm shawl,
Guiding the wanderer lest they should fall.
Through the haze and frost, a light breaks through,
A symbol of courage in a world so blue.

Each night, the stars bow to its gleaming fate,
A promise renewed, never too late.
It whispers of dreams yet to find their way,
In the arms of the night, they long to stay.

As shadows creep in, and darkness takes flight,
It holds the horizon, a guardian of light.
So I follow its glow, my heart intertwined,
With the stories of hope that the beacon designed.

In the heart of the tundra, where silence prevails,
This luminous guide tells forgotten tales.
With every pulse and flicker it sends,
A beacon in the night, as the world transcends.

Frost-Kissed Radiance

A shimmer of ice on the treetops high,
Frost-kissed radiance, under the sky.
Glistening softly, each branch a gem,
In winter's embrace, nature's diadem.

With the dawn breaking gently, a cascade of light,
The world is reborn in a dazzling sight.
Every snowflake dances, every glimmer sings,
Life in the stillness, as the cold breeze clings.

Among frosted fields, the silence profound,
Is a beauty that echoes, a soft, sacred sound.
The radiance sparkles on crystal-tipped grass,
A fleeting moment, but oh how it lasts.

As twilight descends, a canvas unfolds,
With whispers of magic, and stories retold.
Many secrets hidden, yet all can see,
The frost-kissed radiance, wild and free.

In the hush of the night where the cold winds sigh,
The world softly glimmers under starlit sky.
With every heartbeat, let us linger and dream,
In the warmth of the glow, forever to gleam.

Chasing Shadows in the North

Where the northern lights paint the evening sky,
Chasing shadows, the lost wander by.
In the twilight hours, their silhouettes roam,
Seeking the solace, a place to call home.

Each step through the snow leaves whispers of past,
Echoes of stories that forever last.
With every heartbeat, the cold wind sighs,
A dance of uncertainty where hope never dies.

Beneath the stillness, a pulse can be felt,
The warmth within, where true hearts have dwelt.
Shadows may linger, but courage ignites,
In the heart of the night, chasing what's right.

With every flicker, a glimmer unfolds,
Of dreams intertwined in the tales never told.
So onward we journey, with stars lighting our way,
Chasing shadows, until break of day.

Amongst the vastness, where wild echoes sing,
We follow the night, for the warmth it may bring.
In chasing these shadows, with spirit so bright,
We embrace the unknown, guided by light.

Halo of Light over the Icy Plain

A halo shines bright in the cold,
Whispers of warmth, secrets untold.
The stars dance above in the night,
Guiding lost souls with tender light.

Silence blankets the frozen ground,
Nature's hush is the only sound.
Crystals twinkle, pure and clear,
In this calm, there is nothing to fear.

Moonlight spills on the icy crust,
Dreams awaken, in starlight we trust.
The air is crisp, like a sweet embrace,
Filling the heart with tranquil grace.

Shadows linger, shy and slight,
As I wander through the gentle night.
Time stands still as I roam free,
In a world that feels like a symphony.

A halo of light begins to fade,
But memories linger, softly laid.
In the icy plain, hope takes flight,
Bound forever in the glowing night.

The Glow of Dreams in a Frosty World

In a frosty world where dreams ignite,
Colors burst in the silent night.
The glow of wishes fills the air,
Crystals shimmer with tender care.

Each breath forms a cloud, so divine,
As stars align in a cosmic line.
The chill wraps tight, like a soft quilt,
In the silence, all worries wilt.

Footprints left in the sparkling snow,
Lead to a place where heartbeats flow.
Whispers of comfort in the breeze,
Bring forth warmth, like a gentle tease.

The night sky wears a blanket of grace,
With every twinkle, we find our place.
In this dreamscape, we rise and hover,
Connected to each other, like no other.

The glow fades slowly, night's last sigh,
Yet the dreams linger, never die.
In a frosty world, our spirits will play,
Eternal and bright, come what may.

Luminous Pathways of Frost

Luminous pathways weave through the night,
Frost-kissed trails bathe in silver light.
Each step a dream, whispering chance,
Inviting the stars to join the dance.

Cool tendrils of mist curl around,
As night wraps softly, all around.
The world transforms, a glistening sight,
In every corner, magic takes flight.

Guided by glows, we wander far,
Tracing the paths of each shining star.
In this realm, where shadows play,
Hope glimmers bright, lighting the way.

Frozen branches, adorned with pearls,
Echo the tales of forgotten worlds.
In silence, hearts beat, strong and bright,
Following the luminous path of night.

Each moment captured, frozen in time,
Notes of the universe, a gentle rhyme.
We walk together, beneath the dome,
In the frosty glow, we find our home.

A Soft Glow in the Polar Night

A soft glow rests on the icy breath,
Whispers of warmth amidst the depths.
The polar night cradles the land,
In a gentle embrace, peaceful and grand.

The sky paints shades of blue and gold,
Stories of ages silently told.
Beneath the veil, secrets lie deep,
In the soft glow, dreams dare to leap.

Each star twinkles, a distant gleam,
Filling the heart with hope and dream.
As the world sleeps, still and bright,
A soft glow lingers in the night.

Footfalls silent on the snowy white,
Guided by starlight, a sweet delight.
The air, it shimmers with frosty grace,
In this frozen haven, we find our place.

The polar night with its gentle hand,
Holds us tightly in its wondrous land.
With every breath, the glow ignites,
In the heart of winter, love unites.

Beneath the Galactic Ice

Stars whisper secrets, cool and bright,
Cascading shadows, veiling night.
Frozen wonders, silence calls,
Mysteries bound in cosmic halls.

Drifting softly, time stands still,
Galaxies dance with grace and thrill.
Crystals shimmering, vast and grand,
Stories woven in starlit sand.

A blanket deep, an endless sea,
Frozen echoes of what could be.
In silence, dreams begin to grow,
Beneath the ice, the cosmos glows.

With every heartbeat, distance fades,
As light cascades through galactic shades.
Threads of wonder, weaves in space,
Beneath the ice, we find our place.

Hushed Radiance on Still Wings

Gentle breezes brush the trees,
Softly humming, nature's ease.
In twilight's glow, the shadows play,
A world transformed at end of day.

Silence whispers secrets rare,
Feathers glisten in the air.
With every flutter, dreams take flight,
In soft ballet, we chase the light.

Hushed radiance, a soothing balm,
Moments linger, quietly calm.
The moon embraces, night unfolds,
Stories whispered, softly told.

Still wings carry in the night,
Travelers drawn to gentle light.
Each breath a promise, love will sing,
In the hush, our hearts take wing.

Remote Twinkles of Hope

In distant realms, a spark appears,
Whispers flutter across the years.
Fading glimmers, stars alight,
Dreams ignited in the night.

A canvas vast, the cosmos sighs,
Each twinkle hides a thousand tries.
Through shadows deep, we search and seek,
Finding strength in what is weak.

Hope's embrace, a guiding star,
No matter how lost, we wander far.
In the silence, we sow our seeds,
Remote twinkles fulfill our needs.

Light the lanterns, cast your gaze,
A dance of stardust, endless praise.
Embrace the night, let spirits soar,
In these twinkles, we explore.

Frosty Rays in the Twilight

Winter whispers through the trees,
Frosty rays glide on the breeze.
Twilight wraps the world in white,
Painting shadows, soft and light.

Cold embrace, yet hearts will warm,
In quiet moments, find the charm.
Glistening branches, magic grown,
In frosty beauty, we are known.

Last light dances, twinkling bright,
As day surrenders to the night.
Every glimmer, a promise made,
In fleeting colors, dreams won't fade.

Step by step, the night descends,
With every breath, the magic blends.
Frosty rays, a soothing balm,
In twilight's grasp, we find our calm.

Whispering Lights on Frozen Waters

Beneath the stars, the water glows,
Whispers of light as the cold wind blows.
Reflections dance on icy skin,
Nature's secrets lie deep within.

The stillness sings a silent song,
Echoes of dreams where shadows belong.
Flickers of hope in the midnight air,
Guiding the lost, still and bare.

Each shimmer a tale of days gone by,
Fleeting glimpses of how time can fly.
A canvas painted with hues so bright,
In frozen silence, they ignite.

Winter wraps the world in white,
Cradling whispers with soft delight.
The night wears a crown of crystal clear,
While hearts beat softly, calm and near.

Whispering lights on frozen streams,
Awakening long-forgotten dreams.
Like lullabies sung by the night,
They call to the souls lost in flight.

Shimmering Chills of the Night

In the depth of night, the air turns cold,
Whispers of secrets yet to be told.
Shimmering chills dance on the breeze,
Hushed and gentle, like flickering leaves.

Stars twinkle like diamonds far and near,
Beneath the moon's soft, silvery cheer.
Every breath fogs in the still of the hour,
Nature adorned in her frozen power.

The world seems to pause, in awe it stands,
While frost weaves its dance through the lands.
Chills embrace the soul like a sigh,
Reminders of warmth, as winters fly by.

In this quiet realm, wonders ignite,
Souls intertwined in shimmering night.
Mysteries linger in the glow above,
A tapestry woven with hope and love.

Every heartbeat is felt in the freeze,
A symphony played by the sighing trees.
Shimmering chills, a sweet serenade,
In the arms of night, memories cascade.

Beneath the Aurora's Embrace

Beneath the skies of emerald hues,
The night unveils its mystic views.
Flickering lights with grace they weave,
In their splendor, we dare to believe.

The world holds its breath in quiet bliss,
Wrapped in the magic of nature's kiss.
Stars shimmer softly, each one a tale,
Of journeys taken through winds that sail.

In colors bright, the aurora plays,
Painting the night in delicate ways.
Every brushstroke a whispering prayer,
Calling to hearts, lost in despair.

Tales of the ancients, sung by the night,
Flow through the air with a warm light.
Beneath this canvas where dreams take flight,
We find our solace, our spirits ignite.

Embraced by wonders of cosmic grace,
Together we linger, lost in space.
Beneath the aurora's soft, bright glow,
The essence of magic we come to know.

Twilight's Breath on Ice

Twilight whispers, a soft goodbye,
As hues of orange adorn the sky.
The world is painted in shades of gold,
In the embrace of the night, bold and cold.

Each breath of twilight carries the past,
Stories of seasons, shadows cast.
A chill has fallen, crisp and clear,
Echoing dreams that linger near.

The ice glimmers, capturing light,
Reflecting the beauty of fading light.
In this moment, time feels slow,
As stars awaken and soft winds blow.

Nature holds her breath, still and wise,
As twilight dances across the skies.
Every glance reveals a hidden trace,
Of love and longing in every space.

Twilight's breath settles on the ice,
A fleeting moment, so soft, so nice.
In this serene, enchanted scene,
We find the solace, a heart's unseen.

Radiance of the Frozen Expanse

In the stillness, soft and bright,
Crystal shards reflect the light.
Whispers dance upon the breeze,
As nature bows to winter's ease.

Fields of white, a pristine gown,
Underneath the silver crown.
Glistening dreams in each snowflake,
Hold the stories the winds make.

Frozen rivers, still and clear,
Capture echoes we hold dear.
Beneath the sky's vast, starry dome,
Every heart feels the call of home.

Amidst the warmth of fading sun,
Each moment savored, one by one.
The world transformed in tranquil grace,
Within the radiance of this place.

Silent night, a loving stake,
Embracing all for peace's sake.
Underneath the moon's soft gaze,
The frozen expanse, a warm embrace.

Gleaming Trails in the Snow

Footsteps marked on pristine ground,
In the hush, no other sound.
Paths that shimmer in the light,
Guide us through the tranquil night.

Silver shadows, soft and deep,
Guard the secrets that we keep.
Every crunch a story shared,
Tales of wanderers who dared.

Trees adorned with frosted lace,
Nature's art in every space.
Branches bowing to the chill,
Whispers flowing, time stands still.

A symphony of silver beams,
Shattering the night's deep dreams.
We wander forth with hearts aglow,
On these gleaming trails of snow.

Together under starry skies,
We find wonder in our eyes.
Every moment, pure delight,
As we dance in winter's light.

Echoes of Light on Ice

Across the lake, a mirror glows,
Reflections where the stillness flows.
Soft golden hues break through the blue,
A tapestry of evening's hue.

Each step taken, sharp and clear,
Dance of shadows, drawing near.
Echoes whisper through the night,
Stories wrapped in silver light.

Beneath the surface, life does pulse,
Hidden wonders that surprise us.
In this world, so vast and wide,
We explore nature as our guide.

Crystals glimmer, secrets bright,
Enigmas held in quiet night.
Chasing dreams beneath the stars,
A journey free from earthly bars.

Within the silence, hearts ignite,
Filling every void with light.
Frozen moments carved in time,
We behold this world in rhyme.

The Night Sky's Embrace

Veils of stars drape the night,
Kissing earth with softest light.
Twinkling gems in heavens high,
Whispering secrets from the sky.

The moon spills silver on the land,
Guiding dreams with gentle hand.
A canvas painted rich and deep,
Awakens hearts from restful sleep.

Clouds like shadows drift and sway,
As the darkness leads the way.
In this sacred, quiet space,
We find solace in night's embrace.

Time stands still beneath the veil,
Each heartbeat sings a timeless tale.
With every breath, the cosmos hums,
As magic in the stillness comes.

Together in this starry dance,
We surrender to the night's romance.
An endless bond, both near and far,
In the night sky's loving star.

Flares of the Frozen Realm

In the hush of winter's breath,
Flares of orange and gold gleam,
A world cloaked in misty depth,
Where whispers echo like a dream.

Chilling winds through pines do weave,
Dancing shadows, ghostly light,
Nature's magic—hard to believe,
In the heart of a frozen night.

Stars like diamonds softly glow,
Above the ice that glistens bright,
Paths of shimmered frost do show,
Guiding lost souls in their flight.

Crystals spark beneath bright skies,
The moon's reflection dances keen,
In this realm, where silence lies,
A canvas pure and serene.

Flares ignite as day bids farewell,
Painting skies in vibrant hues,
In the frozen lands, a spell,
Hints of magic in the views.

Shiny Paths Through the Wilderness

Beneath thick trees, the sun breaks through,
Shiny paths that twist and wind,
Where every step brings something new,
And nature's secrets, we may find.

Leaves of gold, their edges bright,
Glisten soft in morning's grace,
Each corner turned, a pure delight,
In this enchanting, hidden place.

Streamlets chatter, laugh, and gleam,
As they race on their merry way,
In every moment, a fleeting dream,
Connected in the wild's display.

Hints of color, wildflowers bloom,
Painting gardens on the ground,
Nature's palette dispels all gloom,
In the wilderness, joy is found.

Every creature joins the dance,
In the sunlight, shadows play,
In these paths, we take our chance,
To embrace the wild and stray.

Prismatic Lights at Dusk

When the sun begins to rest,
Prismatic lights fill the sky,
Colors swirl, nature's best,
As day bids a soft goodbye.

Crimson blends with deep indigo,
Painting clouds in vibrant layers,
In this art, emotions flow,
Nature's brush does not wearers.

Stars awake in the twilight,
Shimmering jewels on velvet deep,
As shadows gather, bringing night,
The world beneath begins to sleep.

Glimmers dance on the horizon,
Soft whispers in the cooling air,
The day fades gently, done,
A canvas rich beyond compare.

In the dusk, we find our peace,
In the calm that nighttime brings,
With every color, beauty's lease,
As the world drifts into dreams.

The Dance of Radiant Spheres

In the cosmic sphere they play,
Radiant lights twirl and spin,
A ballet of night and day,
Where the stillness breathes within.

Planets glide in their own time,
Swirling in a dark embrace,
A rhythm marked in perfect rhyme,
Eternity etched in space.

Stars burst forth, a brilliant show,
Each flicker holds a tale untold,
Guiding hearts through the night's flow,
In this dance of ages old.

Galaxies twinkle, vast and wide,
Caught in the cosmic whirl of fate,
In the universe, dreams abide,
In an endless, shimmering state.

With every turn, new paths arise,
As we gaze at this grand ballet,
In wonder, we lift our eyes,
To the dance of spheres at play.

Nightfall's Shimmering Gifts

Soft whispers of the stars appear,
A silver glow, the night draws near.
In twilight's arms, the world stands still,
As shadows dance upon the hill.

Moonbeams weave through branches tall,
While crickets sing a tranquil call.
The sky, a canvas, vast and wide,
Holds secrets of the night inside.

Each twinkle tells a tale so grand,
Of distant worlds, a cosmic band.
Nightfall gifts its magic rare,
In the stillness, hearts laid bare.

With every breath, we dream anew,
Beneath the heavens, deep and true.
Time slows down in evening's glow,
As night unfolds its gentle show.

Embrace the calm, let worries fade,
In night's embrace, peace is made.
For in the dark, we find the light,
A shimmering gift, pure and bright.

Celestial Breath of the North

Whispers ride on icy winds,
A breath of stars, the night rescinds.
From distant realms, the echoes call,
Where northern lights begin to sprawl.

Silent nights, a canvas bare,
Painted skies with magic rare.
Each flicker speaks of ancient lore,
As nature's heart begins to soar.

The chill embraces all in sight,
Yet warms the soul with pure delight.
In every breeze, a story spins,
Of cosmic threads where life begins.

Underneath the vast expanse,
We feel alive, in a trance.
The northern stars, a guiding force,
Illuminate our destined course.

Together we inhale the night,
In every breath, a spark of light.
As celestial whispers softly flow,
Through the tundra, our spirits grow.

Illuminated Silence on the Edge

At twilight's door, silence reigns,
In hushed tones, the world remains.
Where echoes meld with starlit skies,
And time suspends, a sweet surprise.

Each breath we take is softly shared,
In quietude, our hearts laid bare.
The edge of day, where shadows blend,
In the stillness, worries mend.

Whispers of hope brush against skin,
As night unveils where dreams begin.
Along the brink, we find our way,
Through illuminated night and day.

The stars become our guiding light,
In shadows cast by deeper night.
Together we walk, hand in hand,
Toward horizons yet unplanned.

In silence found, we truly gleam,
Within the depths of every dream.
On the edge, where worlds collide,
A tapestry of stars abides.

Frozen Horizons and Flickering Dreams

In frost-kissed air, horizons stretch,
While dreams ignite, and worlds connect.
Beneath the chill, our hopes take flight,
As stars emerge to greet the night.

Frozen landscapes, pure and wide,
Where whispers of adventure bide.
Each flake that falls a promise new,
Of flickering dreams, both bright and true.

We wander through the silver haze,
In the glow of moonlit rays.
With every step, a story grows,
In the realm where courage flows.

The quiet speaks in tones so pure,
An invitation to endure.
In the frozen grasp, we find our way,
To cherish each and every day.

Flickering dreams like candles burn,
In icy winds, we feel the yearn.
Together on this path we roam,
In frozen horizons, we find home.

Glimmers of Peace in Polar Nights

In the stillness of the night,
Stars begin to gently weave,
Whispers of a world so bright,
Calling forth all hearts to believe.

Softly glows the moonlit tide,
Casting shadows long and deep,
Where the frozen secrets hide,
And the ancient spirits sleep.

Frosted breath of winter's grace,
Lingers where the silence reigns,
Every flake finds its own place,
In the quilt of nature's chains.

A dance of lights upon the snow,
Dreams unfold as night passes,
Touching hearts with gentle flow,
In the realm where magic amasses.

Glimmers whisper tales of peace,
In the dark, a softer glow,
Where the burdens of the world cease,
And love's warmth begins to grow.

Enchanted Spirits of the Midnight Sun

When the twilight meets the dawn,
Colors bleed in vibrant sighs,
Spirits dance on emerald lawn,
Underneath the endless skies.

Mystic shadows intertwine,
As daylight starts to soar,
Laughter echoes, pure, divine,
Calling forth the evermore.

Whirling lights in joyous glee,
Painting dreams on velvet air,
Songs of nature, wild and free,
Blend with whispers everywhere.

Radiant hues of amber glow,
Boundless warmth from heaven's seam,
In the glow, the world will flow,
Carried forth in timeless dream.

Enchanted spirits all around,
Guide the hearts to seek and find,
In this beauty, love is found,
With each heartbeat, intertwined.

Snowbound Whispers

Amidst the drifts of white despair,
Voices linger, soft and low,
Every flake a fleeting prayer,
Carried through the chilling blow.

In the hush of winter's grasp,
Silent stories weave and flow,
In each corner, dreams unclasp,
Flowing softly, to and fro.

Beneath the frost, a heartbeat sighs,
Yearning for the warmth of spring,
Hope awakens, never dies,
In the stillness, life will sing.

Snowbound whispers touch the night,
Bringing tales of love and loss,
Every shadow holds a light,
In the depths, we find the gloss.

Nature's clutch, so pure and white,
Wraps our souls in tender care,
Guiding through the darkest night,
With a promise in the air.

Luminous Frost on Disturbed Snow

Glistening across the ground,
Luminous frost shall unveil,
In the stillness, beauty found,
Tales of winter softly tell.

Beneath the layer of pure white,
Lies a canvas, free and bright,
Each disturbance, a tale spun,
In the silence, frosts have won.

Footprints mark the path we take,
An echo of a fleeting day,
In the chill, our dreams awake,
Dancing shadows start to play.

Frosted whispers float and glide,
On the breath of winter's glee,
In the night where hopes abide,
Finding solace, wild and free.

Luminous frost, our hearts ignite,
Painting stories soft and true,
In this realm of fleeting light,
Every moment beckons you.

Celestial Reflections on Snow

Stars shimmer softly on white,
Whispers of night softly ignite.
Moonlight dances on frozen streams,
In nature's hush, we find our dreams.

Footprints trace journeys, so bold,
Secrets of winter quietly told.
Each flake a story, a fleeting light,
Woven together in the still of night.

Glistening frost on silent trees,
Echoes of laughter on the breeze.
In the calm, peace gently flows,
Celestial reflections where beauty grows.

Clouds drift above in shades of gray,
Horizon kissed by the end of day.
Underneath, the world reclines,
Wrapped in the warmth of soft designs.

A canvas bright, untouched by time,
Promises whispered, softly chime.
Each breath a wonder, crisp and clear,
In snowy realms, the heart draws near.

Frigid Beacons of Hope

Amidst the chill, the fires spark,
Guiding souls through the dark.
Each flame a beacon, radiant and bright,
Illuminating paths in the night.

Snowflakes fall in a gentle dance,
In their beauty, we find our chance.
To cherish warmth, to brave the cold,
In every moment, a story unfolds.

Amongst the white, the shadows play,
Drawing lines on the icy array.
But hope shines true in the coldest hour,
A testament to life's vibrant power.

With every heartbeat, the chill subsides,
Frigid night as the heart abides.
Embers flicker, dreams revive,
In the heart's fire, we feel alive.

Amidst the frost, love takes flight,
Embracing dreams in the frosty night.
Frigid beacons, kindled by grace,
Lead us onward to a warm embrace.

Alight in the Icy Breath

The world slows down in frosty air,
Every breath a cloud, a whisper rare.
Icicles hang like jewels bright,
Suspended magic in the night.

With each step, the crunch is sweet,
Nature's symphony beneath our feet.
We walk through shadows, hand in hand,
Sharing warmth in a frozen land.

Beneath the stars, the night unfolds,
Stories of old in silence told.
The moon, a guardian in its flight,
Watching over us, soft and light.

In frozen realms, our spirits sing,
The joy that winter's chill can bring.
Alight in this glittering embrace,
Finding solace, finding grace.

The icy breath, a gentle shroud,
Wraps us close within its crowd.
As dawn breaks clear, let us be bold,
In winter's grasp, our hearts turn gold.

Aurora's Gentle Caress

In the twilight, colors flare,
A dance of light, soft and rare.
Aurora whispers on the white,
Drawing dreams into the night.

With every pulse, the heavens sing,
A symphony of warmth they bring.
Shadows waltz with hues so bright,
Where the stars find their delight.

Each ribbon trails a story spun,
A cosmic journey just begun.
We watch in awe, hearts in sync,
As the colors blend and wink.

Underneath this painted sky,
We drift in wonder, spirits high.
In nature's canvas, pure and vast,
The moment lingers, shadows cast.

Aurora's touch like velvet soft,
In its embrace, we rise aloft.
As night surrenders to dawn's breath,
We find our peace, beyond all death.

Icebound Flickers of Wonder

Beneath the pale moon's glow,
Flickers dance in silence,
Whispers of the frost's embrace,
Nature's quiet guidance.

Crystals hang from branches,
A symphony of bright,
Each step upon the soft snow,
Leads deeper into night.

Frozen rivers sparkle,
Mirrors of the stars,
In this serene enchantment,
We forget our distant scars.

With every breath a puff,
A ghost of warmth released,
Icebound dreams awaken,
In this tranquil feast.

Oh, how the wonder flows,
Through woods and chilling air,
Moments of pure magic,
Nothing can compare.

Wistful Lights in the Winter Woods

Amidst the tall dark pines,
Wistful lights flicker bright,
A glow against the shadows,
Softly breaking night.

Snowflakes twirl like dancers,
In a ballet so divine,
They sprinkle endless wonder,
On the branches, they entwine.

The world feels paused in stillness,
A hushed and sacred space,
Each moment holds a secret,
Wrapped in icy lace.

Crimson berries linger,
In stark contrast found,
Life beneath the winter,
Through silence does abound.

A gentle sighing whispers,
Through woods both deep and wide,
Wistful lights remind us,
Of warmth we hold inside.

The Frosted Glow of Evening

As evening paints the sky,
With strokes of deep indigo,
A frosted glow begins to rise,
A shimmering tableau.

The world wraps in its stillness,
Covered soft in white,
Starlight spills like silver,
On this magical night.

Wind whispers through the willows,
A lullaby so sweet,
While shadows dance in echoes,
Of a heart that skips a beat.

The moon reflects in silence,
Each slumbering embrace,
A canvas of pure wonder,
In this soft, serene space.

With every breath, we treasure,
This glowing, frosted eve,
A timeless stretch of beauty,
In winter's gentle weave.

Crystal Lighthouses of the Snowfield

In the vast white expanse,
Crystal lighthouses stand,
Guiding hearts with their glow,
A signal in the land.

Their towers loom like sentinels,
Against the darkening sky,
Each shimmer holds a story,
Of dreams that float and fly.

Footsteps in the powder,
Lead to pathways bright,
Knowing within each heartbeat,
There's magic in the night.

Frosted brambles glisten,
In the crisp, cold air,
While the silence wraps around,
A gentle, soothing care.

With wonder in our spirits,
We wander, free and bold,
Finding warmth in the beauty,
Of this winter's gold.

Frigid Beacons of Hope

In the stillness of the night,
Stars twinkle, shining bright.
Whispers of dreams take flight,
Guiding souls with their light.

Frost-kissed breath in the air,
A lantern's glow, a silent prayer.
Through the darkness, we dare,
To find warmth, to care.

Snowflakes dance on the breeze,
Nature pauses, then at ease.
Among the trees, memories freeze,
Hope's sweet song, it never leaves.

Each heartbeat echoes the sound,
A promise whispered all around.
Even when the world seems bound,
Hope's beacon can be found.

So let shadows softly fade,
In every heart, dreams are laid.
Beneath the ice, love's cascade,
Frigid beacons are not afraid.

Celestial Wonders Above the Frost

Beneath the cold, a sky so vast,
Stars shimmer like diamonds cast.
Whispers of cosmos unsurpassed,
In the night, the moments last.

Planets glide, a silent dance,
In their presence, we find chance.
Galaxies twirl, a cosmic romance,
Awakening dreams, a sweet trance.

Meteor trails blaze through the dark,
Each flash ignites a hidden spark.
Across the vastness, bright and stark,
Celestial wonders leave their mark.

Frozen earth with a quiet grace,
As starlit beauty fills the space.
Night unfolds its timeless embrace,
Awakening hope in every place.

Above the frost, the heavens sing,
With every note, a new beginning.
In the silence, joy takes wing,
Celestial wonders forever bringing.

Nightfall's Gentle Embrace

As day surrenders to the night,
Soft shadows wrap the world tight.
Whispers weave through fading light,
In nightfall's arms, we find delight.

Stars emerge, one by one,
A tapestry, a moonlit run.
Secrets dwell beneath the sun,
In the hush, our hearts have fun.

Cool breezes caress our skin,
In this stillness, we begin.
With every breath, we let go in,
Nightfall's gentle lull within.

Here, the quiet speaks the loud,
Each star is part of nature's crowd.
In our peace, we feel so proud,
Within night's warmth, we're enshroud.

So let the darkness be our guide,
With every step, we choose to glide.
In night's embrace, we shall abide,
With dreams and hopes forever tied.

Glimmers Beneath the Aurora

In the sky, colors swirl and play,
Ribbons of light in a mystic display.
Nature's palette brightens the gray,
Glimmers beneath the aurora sway.

Whispers of magic fill the air,
Dancing lights, a vibrant flare.
Hearts lift high, shedding despair,
Each glimmer speaks of dreams to share.

Fingers reach for the unknown,
Under the glow, we're not alone.
In this moment, seeds are sown,
Hope's embers in hearts are grown.

Every flicker tells a tale,
Of journeys tried and bonds that prevail.
Unity shines, we are the sail,
Guided by light, we will not fail.

So let the aurora guide our way,
With each step, we dare to stay.
In glimmers bright, we find our play,
A world alive, come what may.

Shining Through the Veil of Winter

In the silence of the night,
Stars twinkle, soft and bright.
Moonlight dances on the snow,
Guiding dreams where whispers flow.

Beneath the sky, a blanket white,
Magic wakes in soft twilight.
Colors hidden, yet they gleam,
Winter's veil conceals the dream.

Footprints fade in frosted air,
Nature sleeps without a care.
Yet beneath the cold, so still,
Life awaits with quiet thrill.

Branches bow with heavy grace,
Graceful lines that time can't erase.
In the hush, the world ignites,
Each breath taken, pure delight.

As dawn breaks with tender light,
Winter moments take to flight.
Shadows dance in warming glow,
Through the veil where dreams still flow.

Tales of Light Among the Ice

Whispers ride the chilly breeze,
Stories told among the trees.
Icicles hang with grace divine,
Glinting shards of cold, they shine.

Beneath the frost, the world renews,
Life encased in winter's hues.
Glimmers echo through the night,
Tales of warmth, the heart's delight.

Every flake a story told,
Moments captured, pure as gold.
Glancing light, a fleeting kiss,
In this realm of icy bliss.

Rivers twinkle, frozen, still,
Silent songs, a winter's thrill.
Nature's canvas, white and bright,
Fills our hearts with purest light.

As the sun begins to rise,
Nature's pulse, where magic lies.
Tales of light, both warm and wise,
Shimmer bright and mesmerize.

Frosted Trails of Radiance

Along the paths of frosted dreams,
Nature weaves her silver seams.
Each step crunches, crisp and clear,
Echoing whispers, winter's cheer.

Tracks that lead to places bright,
Frosted trails bathed in soft light.
Every breath a cloud of grace,
In this enchanted, frozen place.

Branches sway with whispered charms,
Keeping secrets in their arms.
Horizon draped in morning hue,
Frosted trails lead me to you.

In the quiet, life does bloom,
Muffled heartbeats break the gloom.
Radiance sparkles in the air,
Frosted trails, a journey rare.

As the sun climbs, shadows yield,
Nature's beauty softly revealed.
Frosted trails of pure romance,
Guide the dreamers in their dance.

Whispers of Frosted Glow

In the hush of twilight's call,
Whispers fall like gentle snow.
Every flake a story spun,
In the dance, our hearts are won.

Clouds of silver softly play,
Painting night in shades of gray.
Frosted whispers, sweet embraced,
In this quiet, time's erased.

Underneath the starlit sky,
Love ignites, and spirits fly.
Light cascades like falling stars,
In the glow, we mend our scars.

Crystalline dreams in frosted breath,
Glowing softly, life and death.
Every moment, pure and bright,
Whispers of a warm invite.

As dawn breaks with colors bold,
Tales of warmth and love unfold.
Frosted glow wraps us in grace,
In this quiet, sacred space.

A Dance of Icy Embers

In the night where shadows creep,
Flickers of warmth begin to leap.
Around the fire, whispers play,
A dance of embers leads the way.

With every spark, a story told,
Of hearts that burn, and souls so bold.
The chill of night, a soft caress,
As embers glow, we feel the press.

Frosted air, a gentle sigh,
In this warmth, we learn to fly.
The wind may howl, but here we stay,
In this dance, we find our way.

The flickering light, a tender trace,
In icy shadows, we find our grace.
As night fades into morning bright,
We hold the embers, hearts alight.

Against the chill, we stand our ground,
In unity, our strength is found.
A dance of icy embers bold,
In stories shared, our warmth unfolds.

Crystal Glow in the Stillness

Underneath the silver moon,
A world of crystals hums a tune.
In the stillness, magic flows,
A gentle light, the beauty grows.

Every flake a diamond bright,
Dances softly in the night.
Whispers weave through frosty trees,
Carried on the winter's breeze.

In this landscape, silence reigns,
Peace envelops, soothes the chains.
Amidst the glow, shadows play,
As night holds on to the day.

Crystals glisten, breathless spark,
Painting beauty in the dark.
In their shimmer, dreams take flight,
Guided by the soft moonlight.

The stillness sings, a lullaby,
As night unfurls its velvet sky.
In crystal glow, we find our peace,
In winter's heart, our cares release.

Radiant Echoes of Winter

In frosted fields where silence sings,
Winter weaves its magic strings.
Echoes of a distant past,
In radiant beauty, dreams are cast.

The sun dips low, a golden hue,
Painting landscapes crisp and new.
Footprints shine on fresh white snow,
Stories linger, softly flow.

Whispers travel on the breeze,
Carrying secrets through the trees.
A tender moment, time stands still,
In winter's grasp, we feel the thrill.

Reflections dance on icy streams,
Awakening forgotten dreams.
With every breath, the world ignites,
In radiant echoes, we find our lights.

The heart of winter holds its glow,
Lessons learned through fields of snow.
As days grow short and nights, serene,
In echoes whisper, our souls convene.

The Luminous Tundra

Across the tundra, shadows roam,
A world transformed, a frozen home.
Beneath the stars, the silence deep,
In luminous dreams, the wild ones leap.

The canvas glows with shades so rare,
A painter's touch in the crisp air.
With each new dawn, colors blend,
A shimmering tapestry without end.

Footsteps mark the journey bold,
In landscapes vast, stories unfold.
A polar dance, a fleeting glance,
In the chill, we take our chance.

The night sky blazes with cosmic light,
Guiding hearts through the endless night.
In the expanse where echoes sing,
The tundra whispers, winter's king.

As dawn awakens, warmth will rise,
In bracing winds, an ancient sigh.
The luminous tundra, a sacred space,
Where every heart finds its place.

Ethereal Glows in the Clicking Cold

In the hush of winter's breath,
Ethereal lights begin to play.
Whispers of warmth in the icy depths,
Glistening dreams fade into gray.

Stars dip low to kiss the frost,
While shadows dance in spectral light.
Hope flickers where the lost are tossed,
A fleeting glimpse in the endless night.

Icicles shimmer, a crystal choir,
Singing songs of the silent trees.
Hearts ignite with a gentle fire,
Bound together by winter's freeze.

Through the cold, we find our way,
Guided by the beauty we see.
In the ether where the spirits play,
We forge our dreams, wild and free.

Twilight Sparks Over the Ice

Underneath a dusk-lit sky,
Twilight ignites like a thousand stars.
Golden sparks as the world sighs,
Filling the night with radiant scars.

Ice mirrors the palette of light,
Reflecting hues of crimson and blue.
Nature's canvas, a wondrous sight,
Whispers of magic in every hue.

Frozen whispers dance through the air,
As shadows blend with the coming night.
In the chill, a secret we share,
Embracing the warmth of the fading light.

Winds carry tales of the old,
Of paths laid down by love's embrace.
In twilight's grip, the shy and bold,
Find solace in this blissful space.

Secrets of Light in the Barren Lands

In the vastness where shadows dwell,
Secrets of light break the void.
Amidst the barren, a tranquil spell,
Each flicker of hope, never destroyed.

A whispering beam holds the night,
Breaching silence with radiant grace.
Shapes emerge in the shimmering light,
Painting dreams on this empty space.

Wonders awaken as darkness fades,
In the heart of the frozen ground.
Where each flash of brilliance parades,
The beauty of existence is found.

Together we tread this glowing plain,
Chasing shadows of what has been.
In the vastness, we hold no pain,
For in our hearts, light's always seen.

Radiant Spirits in the Silent Snow

In the stillness where shadows creep,
Radiant spirits begin to rise.
Snowflakes fall, their secrets keep,
Whispers echo in starry skies.

With each breath, the world holds tight,
Wrapped in blankets of glimmering white.
In winter's grasp, a pure delight,
Hearts illuminate the tranquil night.

Figures dance in the frosty air,
Enticing dreams with every swirl.
Magic unravels beyond compare,
As silver stars begin to twirl.

In the silence, we feel the pulse,
Of the earth beneath gentle snow.
Radiant spirits coax us to suss,
The beauty in every silent glow.

Icebound Dreams in Dim Light

In twilight's grasp, the shadows play,
Frozen whispers in the night sway.
Stars glimmer like frost-kissed jewels,
As the world sleeps, wrapped in cool rules.

A silver moon casts a gentle beam,
Through icy branches, it weaves a dream.
Silent sounds like echoes of cheer,
In the chill, our hearts draw near.

Through frosted glass, visions unfold,
Of adventures in lands untouched, bold.
Voices of the winter wind sigh,
As snowflakes dance from the sky.

Each breath visible, a puff of white,
In this stillness, hearts take flight.
Roaming softly, with hope as our guide,
In the shiver of night, dreams abide.

As dawn breaks, the world wakes anew,
With icebound dreams born from the blue.
They linger softly, like a sweet song,
In the dim light, we all belong.

Glowing Whispers of the Tundra

Beneath the stars, the tundra sleeps,
Shrouded in silence, secrets it keeps.
A soft glow emanates from the ground,
In the stillness, magic is found.

Gentle whispers weave through the frost,
Echoes of laughter, never lost.
The auroras dance in hues of gold,
Tales of the earth, silently told.

As shadows lengthen, colors ignite,
A canvas of dreams in the heart of night.
The chill wraps around, a tender embrace,
In nature's arms, we find our place.

The breath of the wild paints the air,
With every heartbeat, freedom we share.
The tundra's spirit, wild and free,
Whispers to souls, come dance with me.

When dawn unfolds, the colors fade,
Yet the memories last, never betrayed.
In glowing whispers, we find our way,
To carry their warmth through each day.

Dancing Lights in the Wilderness

In the wilderness, the night is bright,
Dancing lights ignite the sky's height.
Nature's spectacle, a radiant show,
Whispers of magic in the wind flow.

Among the trees, shadows sway,
As the stars join in this playful ballet.
With every flicker, stories arise,
Of ancient tales beneath the skies.

The crackle of fire, a heartbeat's tune,
Illuminates faces, like the moon.
In this moment, we are alive,
With dancing lights, our spirits thrive.

Laughter mingles with the night air,
Echoing softly, without a care.
In the embrace of the wild and free,
We find our joy, our symphony.

As dawn approaches, lights may wane,
Yet the magic lingers, sweet as rain.
In the wilderness, our hearts unite,
As we dance with the stars, in the night.

A Symphony of Frost and Fire

In the chill of night, a symphony starts,
Frost and fire weave through our hearts.
With crackling embers and icy breath,
We find beauty within fleeting death.

The warmth of the flames, a bright refrain,
As the wind carries whispers of pain.
Yet in this contrast, we find delight,
Crafting tales in the depths of night.

Like crystal notes in a winter's air,
Each moment precious, beyond compare.
As frost paints the world in shimmering white,
Firelight holds us close, warm and bright.

The dance of duality, fire and ice,
Creating a harmony, a paradise.
In the stillness, we hear the call,
Of a symphony that unites us all.

When morning breaks and shadows flee,
The memories linger, wild and free.
In the heart's chamber, they softly play,
A symphony cherished, come what may.

Guiding Lights in the Chill

Through the frost, soft whispers call,
Stars above like candles fall,
In the dark, their glow so bright,
Leading souls through endless night.

Icicles hang, a crystal dance,
In their gaze, we find romance,
Each twinkling spark a hopeful sign,
Guiding hearts to dreams divine.

Moonlit paths weave through the trees,
Carrying secrets on the breeze,
Each shadow cast, a fleeting guide,
In this chill, we choose to bide.

Frosted breath in the silent air,
With each step, we shed the care,
Flickering lights, a warm embrace,
Time slows down in this sacred space.

In the night, each flicker glows,
Where the chilly river flows,
Together we find hope anew,
In guiding lights, our spirits view.

Shards of Light in the Silence

In the quiet, shadows kneel,
Shards of light begin to feel,
Splintered beams that spark our trust,
In the stillness, dreams combust.

Voices whisper through the night,
Echoing in soft twilight,
Every shimmer tells a tale,
Of courage found when spirits pale.

Glimmers dance on hidden streams,
Lighting up our fractured dreams,
In the hush, we take a stand,
Shards of hope lend us a hand.

Fragments catch the evening glow,
Softly guiding where to go,
Lost in time's embrace, we find,
Light and silence intertwined.

In each shadow, brilliance lies,
Reflecting truth in velvet skies,
Embrace the shards that gently gleam,
In the silence, we can dream.

Illuminating the White Vastness

Across the fields, the white expanse,
Light cascades in a soft dance,
Every flake a sparkling prayer,
Illuminating without a care.

Mountains rise like silent guards,
In their shadows, dreams are stars,
Snowflakes fall, a gentle touch,
Wrapping earth in warmth and hush.

In this endless snowy sea,
Where silence breathes tranquility,
The sun's embrace, a radiant spark,
Guides us through the quiet dark.

Whispers echo through the time,
In this realm, we find the rhyme,
With every step, a moment's grace,
In the vastness, we embrace.

Illuminated paths unfold,
In the white, our hearts behold,
Together we chase the light's dance,
In the vastness, we take a chance.

Glacial Glows

In the chill of twilight's beam,
Glacial glows begin to dream,
Frozen rivers sing their song,
In their depths, we linger long.

Crystals form in whispered light,
Dancing softly in the night,
Each facet tells of time so old,
Stories waiting to be told.

Beneath the surface, secrets dwell,
In the stillness, all is well,
Illumination cold yet kind,
In glacial hearts, peace we find.

With every breath, the world awakens,
In its beauty, joy unshaken,
Moments freeze in twilight's hold,
In glacial glows, our dreams unfold.

Through the night, we wander free,
Chasing lights, our spirits flee,
Glacial glows, a guiding light,
In the darkness, hope takes flight.

Flickers in the Frost

In the dawn's soft glow, flickers flare,
Gentle whispers dance through chilled air.
Each crystal bright, a fleeting sight,
In winter's breath, pure and light.

Branches bow low, a silver quilt,
Nature's art, with grace is built.
Frosted edges, a delicate line,
A world reborn, pure and divine.

Echoes of cold in tranquil night,
Stars above gleam with quiet light.
A hush envelops, time stands still,
As dreams awaken, hearts they fill.

Softly we tread, on ground of white,
Each step a whisper, pure delight.
The chill embraces, tender and true,
In every flicker, life anew.

Twinkling gems on nature's stage,
Bringing forth wisdom of every age.
The frosty breath of winter's kiss,
In its caress, we find our bliss.

Celestial Gleams of Ice

Under twilight's veil, the stars ignite,
Celestial gleams in the still of night.
Each glimmering shard, a story untold,
Frozen wonders in silver and gold.

The moon casts shadows, a soft embrace,
As icy fingers weave through space.
Whispers of cosmos, bright and clear,
Call to our hearts, so close, so near.

A tapestry spun from frosty mists,
Intertwined fates that fate insists.
Through shimmering pathways, we are led,
To dreams of the frozen stars ahead.

Each twinkle beckons with promise bright,
Illuminating the depths of night.
Beneath the veil of ice and snow,
The beauty whispers, sweet and slow.

In silence we marvel, in wonder we find,
The universe's secrets, gently aligned.
As celestial gleams start to fade,
Hope lingers on, never betrayed.

Whispered Light on Polar Winds

In the arctic embrace, whispers flow,
Light dances softly, a gentle glow.
Polar winds sing, a soothing tune,
Under the watch of the silver moon.

Snowflakes twirl, like dreams that soar,
Each flake a promise, forevermore.
The icy breath caresses the trees,
Carrying stories on the breeze.

Silent echoes in the shimmering night,
Whispered warmth in the heart of the light.
Where shadows play, and spirits chase,
In every corner, find a space.

A canvas of stars, a palette of dreams,
Reflecting the beauty in delicate beams.
Through crystal paths, we wander far,
Guided by whispers, beneath the stars.

In the frost's embrace, we find our way,
As whispered light leads us to stay.
With open arms and hopeful hearts,
In every breath, the magic starts.

Shimmering Stars Beneath the Snow

Beneath the blanket of soft, white snow,
Shimmering stars in the moonlight glow.
Hidden treasures, waiting to be found,
In winter's hush, magic abounds.

Each flake reflects distant dreams,
The universe whispers through frozen streams.
With every drift, stories unfold,
Of time and space, both timeless and bold.

Enchanted silence wraps the land,
While shimmering stars take a graceful stand.
With hearts entwined, we seek the light,
Amidst the wonder of the quiet night.

Memories dance on a glistening breeze,
With softly spoken secret pleas.
As winter's magic weaves through the air,
A tapestry rich beyond compare.

In every corner where shadows play,
Shimmering stars lead the way.
Beneath the snow, the world holds its breath,
In quiet beauty, life conquers death.

Nature's Guiding Glow Among the Pines

In shadows deep, the sunlight weaves,
Through emerald branches, whispers of leaves.
A gentle breeze sings lullabies,
While nature's glow enchants our eyes.

Golden rays dance on forest floor,
Inviting footsteps to explore.
Each rustling leaf tells ancient tales,
Of whispered winds and hidden trails.

Majestic pines stand tall and proud,
Guardians of secrets, wrapped in a shroud.
They shelter dreams beneath their might,
Cradled softly in the fading light.

Sparkling dew adorns the dawn,
As the world awakens, gently drawn.
Nature's heartbeat in every beat,
Guiding us where earth and sky meet.

In this serene and sacred place,
We find the peace of nature's grace.
Among the pines, our spirits soar,
In nature's glow, we seek for more.

Ghostly Flames in the Polar Night

In polar realms where silence reigns,
The ghostly flames cast eerie stains.
Dancing shadows, flickering bright,
Illuminate the endless night.

Stars above, like diamonds twine,
With whispers soft, your heart aligns.
The aurora paints the frigid air,
With colors vivid, beyond compare.

Glacial winds carry tales untold,
Of ancient spirits, daring and bold.
In frozen landscapes, magic thrives,
As mystery and wonder survives.

Crisp and clear, the night so still,
Where echoes of the past fulfill.
In ghostly flames, we find our way,
Through shadowed dreams that softly sway.

With each flicker, a memory glows,
Of frozen worlds, where legend flows.
In polar night, our souls ignite,
By ghostly flames, our hearts take flight.

Shards of Light on Icy Paths

In winter's chill, where shadows lay,
Icy paths reflect the day.
Shards of light, like crystal tears,
Guide our steps through fleeting years.

Glittering frost on ancient stones,
Echoes of whispers, winter's tones.
Each glimmer speaks of time gone by,
Of memories etched beneath the sky.

Footprints linger, soft and small,
In nature's grip, we feel it all.
A journey marked by fleeting light,
On icy paths in the stillness of night.

With every step, a story unfolds,
In radiant shards, the heart beholds.
Nature's beauty, stark and true,
In icy trails, we find what's due.

Among the frost, we walk our way,
In search of warmth, of hope, of day.
Shards of light illuminate the dark,
Guiding us gently, leaving a mark.

Chilled Whispers from the Hearth

In the ashes, warmth resides,
Chilled whispers of the night abides.
The crackling fire sings of home,
In flickering light, our spirits roam.

Outside, the frost bites cold and keen,
But here, the hearth glows warm and serene.
Embers dance with tales to share,
Of joy and sorrow, moments rare.

Wrapped in blankets, tales we weave,
As haunted wind beckons to leave.
The hearth, a friend in winter's chill,
Offers comfort, quiet and still.

Each whisper carried on the breeze,
Invites us back to hearts at ease.
In this embrace, we find delight,
In chilled whispers that pierce the night.

Together, we craft our dreams anew,
By fireside glow, with warmth infused.
Chilled whispers from the hearth we share,
In love and laughter, beyond compare.

Aurora's Silent Flame

In the stillness of the night,
Colors dance in soft delight.
Whispers of the northern light,
Awakening the sky's own plight.

A canvas painted in hues bold,
Secrets of the night unfold.
Through the darkness, stories told,
In a symphony of gold.

Silent flames that flicker bright,
Guiding dreams with gentle light.
Hearts embraced in vibrant flight,
Lost in a moment, pure and right.

Each shimmer holds a tale untold,
Traces of the brave, the cold.
With every brush, a memory scrolled,
A universe of wonder, controlled.

From twilight's cusp to dawn's sweet kiss,
In this realm, we find our bliss.
Holding on to starlit wishes,
Nothing fades, love's warmth persists.

Chasing Shimmering Shadows

In the fields where shadows play,
Whispers of the fading day.
Chasing dreams that slip away,
Echoes of the past, they sway.

Fleeting glimpses, soft and shy,
Flickers of a forgotten sky.
We reach out, we question why,
As silhouettes whisper goodbye.

Each step taken, paths entwine,
Ghostly figures, lost in time.
Shimmering trails, a dance so fine,
In pursuit of moments divine.

Through the meadows, footsteps light,
Chasing shadows into night.
With every breath, a silent fight,
To hold the dreams just out of sight.

Yet in shadows, we find grace,
A fleeting glance, a soft embrace.
In chasing light, we set our pace,
Forever drawn to time and space.

Lights Beneath the Polar Skies

Beneath the vast and icy dome,
Whispers of the night find home.
Stars adorned in shimmering tome,
Guiding hearts that roam and roam.

In frozen lands, the magic grows,
A symphony in chilly throes.
Ah, the lights, how brightly they pose,
Telling tales that nature knows.

Glistening like diamonds in the dark,
Every twinkle leaves a mark.
In the silence, hear the spark,
Of distant dreams that start to hark.

A dance of colors, bold and free,
Painting the skies, a jubilee.
Underneath, we dare to be,
Lost in wonder, you and me.

With every rise of dawn's embrace,
Memories etched in this place.
Beneath the skies, in time and space,
The lights remain, our sacred grace.

Frostbitten Dreams

In dreams that chill the bones at night,
Frostbitten whispers take their flight.
Figures dance in silver light,
Leaving traces of their plight.

Shadows creep on frozen ground,
In silence, all our hopes are found.
Through the mist, the past resounds,
Frostbitten echoes, tightly bound.

Each breath a cloud, soft and white,
In the stillness, hearts ignite.
With every flicker, we invite,
The warmth of memories in sight.

A tapestry of stars up high,
Kissed by dreams that dare to fly.
In these realms, we seek to pry,
Hidden truths that never die.

So hold the frost within your palm,
Embrace the chill, the quiet calm.
In dreams, we find a timeless balm,
Frostbitten, but our hearts are warm.

Northern Radiance

In the hush of the night, soft lights play,
Whispers of magic in the sky, they sway.
Each twinkle a story, each shimmer a dream,
Painting the heavens with a silvery gleam.

Winds carry echoes of ancient delight,
Dancing through shadows, embracing the night.
Stars weave a tapestry, endless and bright,
Guiding lost travelers with their gentle light.

Mountains stand guard, cloaked in pure white,
Reflecting the brilliance of the dazzling sight.
Nature's own lanterns, fierce and serene,
Watch over the world in a glistening sheen.

Silent and ageless, the auroras will flow,
Ribbons of colors in a graceful show.
Wrap them in warmth, let your worries take flight,
Embrace the enchantment of Northern Radiance's light.

Hold close the moments, feel the deep peace,
In this realm of wonder, let your heart cease.
For in every flicker, a message is sent,
A blessing of beauty, a soul's firmament.

Glimmering Ice Echoes

Amidst the stillness, ice crystals gleam,
In the heart of winter, a silent dream.
Frosted whispers glide on the evening's breath,
Painting the landscape, a portrait of death.

Beneath the moon's gaze, silvered and bright,
Echoes of shadows dance in the night.
Nature's symphony in chilling refrain,
Melodies linger, long after the pain.

Footsteps imprint on the soft, powdery layer,
Each mark a remembrance, a fading prayer.
The chill of the night wraps tightly around,
Bearing the secrets of distant, cold sound.

With every breath taken, the air turns to gold,
As stories of winter timelessly unfold.
Glimmers of light pierce through the abyss,
In this world of ice, find warmth in the bliss.

So listen closely, as silence will speak,
Of dreams held within every frosted peak.
The echo of glimmers, forever in sight,
Lingers in shadows, of Glimmering Ice Night.

Celestial Luminaries

High above us, the stars swirl and spin,
Celestial guardians, where dreams begin.
Each point of light like a wish on the air,
A promise of hope that whispers a prayer.

In the vast canvas where galaxies glide,
Cosmic marvels, in silence, they bide.
Through the void of night, they boldly ignite,
Carrying souls on wings of pure light.

Planets in motion, pulsing with grace,
Eclipsing the darkness, they claim their place.
Constellations twinkle, forming a map,
Leading the dreamers out of their trap.

Feel the allure of the infinite skies,
In their embrace, let your spirit rise.
Among the celestial, a heart found anew,
As Luminaries guide and illuminate you.

With every heartbeat, the cosmos will hum,
In tune with the universe, see how we come.
For in this vast expanse, we are never alone,
In the dance of the stars, we find our true home.

Frozen Beacons of Night

In the darkened silence, a glow starts to rise,
Frozen beacons scatter, lighting the skies.
Each flicker a promise, a flicker of hope,
In the depths of winter, we learn how to cope.

The moon drapes her silver o'er landscape so wide,
Casting shadows that shimmer, with nowhere to hide.
Underneath this blanket of stillness and light,
Our dreams take their flight, through the cold, endless night.

With whispers of frost, the cool breezes tell,
Tales of the ancients, where twilight fell.
Stars like sentinels, guard the night's flight,
Frozen beacons beckon, guiding us right.

Embrace the stillness, let the silence flow,
For in the deep night, life's mysteries grow.
These shimmering treasures, each glowing delight,
Illuminate paths through the heart's hidden fright.

So revel in beauty, in the chill of the air,
Find solace in whispers that drift everywhere.
In Frozen Beacons, our spirits unite,
A chorus of wonders, in the depths of the night.

Celestial Snowflakes

In the night sky, they softly fall,
Each unique flake, a crystal call.
Whispers of winter, gentle and pure,
Dancing down, a frosty allure.

Drifting silently, they blanket the ground,
Softening edges, a hush all around.
Under the moonlight, they gleam so bright,
Creating a wonder, a magical sight.

Touched by the winds, they twirl and spin,
Gathering secrets where dreams begin.
A kingdom of white, in silence they reign,
Each flake a story, a glimpse of the lane.

In the early morn, they catch the first light,
Transforming the world, from dark into bright.
Celestial wonders, so fleeting and fast,
Reminding us always, that moments don't last.

With every snowfall, the world is renewed,
A dance of the heavens, in pure solitude.
Celestial snowflakes, in beauty they blend,
A journey of peace that never will end.

Luminous Secrets of the Glaciers

Beneath the blue, where shadows reside,
Luminous secrets in ice do confide.
Whispers of ages, they softly convey,
The tales of the earth in shades of gray.

Crystalline echoes of times long past,
In frozen depths, memories cast.
Melodies trapped in a shimmering dance,
Each crack and crevice, a timeless romance.

Glistening surfaces that shimmer and glow,
Guarding the wonders that few ever know.
Serenading silence, the ice holds its breath,
A sanctuary blessed, confronting the death.

As seasons shift, and the glaciers weep,
The stories unfold, in shadows they seep.
Luminous secrets, both awe and fright,
Reflections of nature, pure and bright.

In twilight's embrace, the glaciers ignite,
A canvas of secrets under moonlight.
Painting the world with a soft, gentle brush,
Luminous visions that make our hearts rush.

Flickering Hopes in the Frost

In the chill of the night, a whispering glow,
Flickering hopes where the cold winds blow.
Dreams intertwining in frosty despair,
Lighting a path through the still, frigid air.

Frost-kissed shadows dance 'neath the stars,
Each shimmering spark tells tales from afar.
In the heart of the winter, a flickering fire,
Kindling the souls with a passionate desire.

Gathering warmth from a memory's thread,
Flickering hopes where the heart is led.
With every soft sigh, a promise in sight,
The frost may be fierce, but hope shines so bright.

Moments of stillness, thoughts weave and thread,
Creating a tapestry where dreams are fed.
Among the white silence, a heartbeat remains,
Flickering hopes, like a sweet summer rain.

With every bold step on the frostbitten ground,
Strength blooms in shadows, in silence profound.
Flickering hopes will dance through the night,
Carving paths forward to embrace the light.

Frosted Glimmers of Solitude

In a world wrapped in a silvery sheen,
Frosted glimmers of solitude gleam.
The quiet prevails, as day turns to night,
Embracing the stillness, a delicate light.

With every breath, the cold air ignites,
A canvas of wonders in shadowy heights.
Each frost-laden branch tells tales untold,
Awakening dreams in the bitter cold.

The solitude whispers, a soft, gentle hum,
In the deepest of winter, a stillness that comes.
Frosted glimmers where silence does sing,
Cradling the heart in the warmth of a spring.

Amidst the white beauty, reflection takes flight,
Frosted glimmers guiding us through the night.
Moments of peace, as a soft flake does land,
Creating a sanctuary, where dreams take a stand.

In the hush of the evening, tranquility reigns,
Frosted glimmers weaving through joy and pains.
In solitude found, a treasure unfolds,
A heart touched by winter, in silence enfolds.

Glacial Wonders Towards Infinity

Icicles hanging, sharp and bright,
Mirrored surfaces catch the light.
Frozen winds whisper secrets low,
In this realm where cold winds blow.

Mountains rise with icy grace,
Carved by time in this vast space.
Crystals dance in the moon's soft gaze,
Guiding dreams through winter's haze.

Hearts entwined in frosty air,
Find solace in moments rare.
Every breath a fleeting sigh,
Underneath the endless sky.

Beneath the stars, glimmers vast,
Nature's beauty, unsurpassed.
In silence deep, we find our way,
To watch the night erase the day.

Infinite wonders, bold and pure,
Through glacial paths, we will endure.
With each step, the journey's song,
Echoes where the hearts belong.

Ethereal Sparks in the Polar Void

In the stillness, colors dance,
Amidst the frost, a fleeting chance.
Northern lights weave stories bright,
Fleeting dreams take off in flight.

Silent whispers fill the night,
As stars flicker with pure delight.
Ethereal sparks in icy air,
Draw us closer, a magnetic snare.

Celestial wonders swirl and sway,
Guiding spirits on their way.
In the polar void, we are found,
In the magic all around.

Time stands still in this frozen place,
Every heartbeat, a tranquil grace.
The universe hums a quiet tune,
Underneath the watchful moon.

As we wander through the white,
Embraced by the ethereal light.
In the stillness, we are one,
Bound by dreams, the journey's begun.

Flickers in the Vast White

Snowflakes drift in carefree flight,
Painting landscapes pure and bright.
In quiet moments, flickers glow,
Stories whispered in the snow.

Footsteps crunch on icy ground,
Echoes of the world surround.
A playful breeze begins to tease,
As winter wakes with gentle ease.

Horizon stretches, vast and wide,
Underneath the stormy tide.
Flickers of hope shine through the chill,
Filling hearts with dreams to fulfill.

As the sky holds shades of grey,
Resilient spirits find their way.
Through the frozen, vast expanse,
We find joy in winter's dance.

Flickers of warmth in icy nights,
Guiding us to boundless heights.
In the vast white, we find our song,
Embracing where we all belong.

Reflections of a Frozen Star

In twilight's glow, a star descends,
Casting shadows, a tale it sends.
Reflections shimmer on the ice,
Whispers of fate in every slice.

The night embraces the frozen ground,
Where secrets of time can be found.
Glimmers of light through depths of cold,
Eternal stories gently told.

Stars above, like diamonds bright,
Dance with dreams in endless night.
Every flicker holds a trace,
Of warmth in this frigid space.

As silence reigns, hearts resonate,
In harmony with night so great.
Reflections in the crystal clear,
Embrace the magic that brings us near.

Underneath the frozen sky,
We share our hopes and dreams that fly.
Reflections of a star so grand,
Guide us gently, hand in hand.

Luminous Threads of Arctic Winds

Beneath the dance of northern lights,
The winds weave tales of icy nights.
Each breath a whisper, soft and clear,
A melody only the brave can hear.

Snowflakes twirl in silent grace,
A shimmering quilt that time can't chase.
The forests stand like sentinels tall,
Guarding secrets in winter's thrall.

With every gust, a story flows,
Of ancient paths where time ebbs slow.
The echoes of nature, wild and free,
Cocooned in frost, longing to be.

In twilight's hue, the landscape sighs,
A canvas painted 'neath starry skies.
The arctic air, sharp yet sweet,
Transforms the world beneath our feet.

Through the night, a shimmer spreads,
A tapestry where dreams are bred.
In luminous threads of frozen breath,
Life dances boldly with the death.

Frigid Stars in a Pastel Sky

In the hush of dusk, the colors blend,
Pastel hues where shadows bend.
Frigid stars begin to gleam,
Whispering softly, a cosmic dream.

Ice-capped peaks catch the fading light,
Sentinels guarding the coming night.
The sky wraps dusk in a delicate lace,
As time pauses in this frozen space.

Glistening crystals adorn the ground,
In silence, beauty can be found.
Each breath a cloud in the chilling air,
Binding us all with secrets rare.

Amidst the quiet, the world transforms,
Nature's palette, a beauty that warms.
Frigid stars twinkle their ancient tales,
Guiding wanderers across icy trails.

Beneath the canvas of this pastel dome,
The heart finds solace, a sense of home.
In the calm of night, we quietly sigh,
Beneath the frigid stars in a pastel sky.

Whispered Secrets in Glacial Light

In glacial light, the world refracts,
Secrets of ages in silence stacked.
With every glimmer, truths unfold,
Stories of warmth in the depths of cold.

Rivers of ice, they twist and turn,
In their flow, a lesson to learn.
Mountains cradle the whispers' flight,
Guarding memories shrouded in white.

Beneath the surface, life endures,
In frozen realms, the heart ensures.
Translucent layers, a delicate shroud,
Promising peace, both silent and loud.

Through valleys deep, the shadows creep,
Yet the shimmer of hope, it brightly leaps.
In every cranny, a flicker ignites,
Illuminating dreams on forgotten nights.

In the embrace of glacial glow,
A wisdom that only the ancients know.
With whispered secrets, the winds ignite,
The beauty of truths in glacial light.

Faint Glows of Forgotten Skies

In dusk's embrace, the horizon sighs,
Whispers of yesteryears in forgotten skies.
Faint glows flicker like distant stars,
Echoing symphonies, playing soft guitars.

Beneath the veil of twilight's embrace,
Time meanders in a gentle chase.
Shadows linger where memories dwell,
In every heartbeat, a story to tell.

Clouds drift lazily, painting the air,
With each stroke, leaving tales laid bare.
Colors merge, a soft requiem,
Composed by nature, a silent hymn.

The night beckons with secrets old,
In its arms, all futures unfold.
In the quiet glow, we find our place,
A union of dreams, a fleeting grace.

Faint glows rise as the past entwines,
Illuminating paths like constellations' signs.
In forgotten skies, we lose and find,
The echoes of love that space left behind.

Enchanted Luminescence on Bitter Winds

In the night, shadows dance and sway,
Whispers of frost in the air softly play.
Glimmers of warmth in the cold winds cry,
Stars weave stories as they twinkle high.

Moonlight drapes the earth in silver lace,
Carving out dreams in a tranquil space.
Each flicker speaks of a world's embrace,
Nature's rhythm, a celestial race.

Bitter winds may howl with icy breath,
Yet in their song, we find life and death.
For every chill, a fire's glow will rise,
Guided by hope, we follow the skies.

Enchanted whispers carry through the night,
Holding the secrets of shadow and light.
With every breath, the universe sings,
Awakening joy that the starlight brings.

In this embrace, all the pain shall cease,
Mending the hearts, inviting the peace.
As night graces dawn, a new day shall start,
Binding the cosmos within every heart.

Mirage of Light in the Chill

A flicker of hope in the gloaming light,
Dancing reflections take flight in the night.
The air is crisp, with a promise unspun,
Mirrored visions of warmth from the sun.

Through the canvas of dusk, hues intertwine,
Painting the horizon with brushes divine.
Every breath forms a cloud in the air,
Each moment lingers, vibrant and rare.

Caught in the glow of a phantom parade,
Chilled by the breeze, yet never dismayed.
The spirit embraces the bittersweet song,
In this mirage, we continue along.

As shadows retreat, the chill will remain,
Yet in the twilight, we break from the chain.
Reveling in warmth from memories kept,
Dancing in light, where our dreams have wept.

With each flicker, a wish shall ignite,
In the heart of the void, we find our delight.
Amidst the cold, let the warmth arise,
For in every spark, the dreamer still tries.

Shimmering Hues of the Northern Sky

Beneath the canopy of twinkling stars,
Colors awaken, like distant guitars.
Crimson and blue in the twilight's hold,
Stories unfold in the night, brave and bold.

Ripples of light in a luminous sea,
Whispering secrets of what's yet to be.
Nature's palette, a wondrous display,
Guiding lost souls as they wander their way.

Emerald shades blend with sapphire deep,
In shimmering hues, the cosmos does weep.
With every flicker, the spirits unite,
Painting the darkness, igniting the light.

In the silence, we feel a heartbeat,
Music of stars, a celestial feat.
Embracing the charm of this astral dome,
Every shimmering hue calls us back home.

The northern sky holds each dream we weave,
In luminous threads that we dare to believe.
And as we gaze at the vastness so wide,
A world of wonders unfolds by our side.

Twilight's Soft Embrace

In twilight's glow, the day starts to fade,
Softly the shadows weave pathways made.
Whispers of dusk float on gentle wind,
Hearts find solace, where dreams rescind.

The colors blend, a painter's delight,
Fading to twilight, softly taking flight.
A canvas alive with the chill of the night,
Guiding our souls to the stars burning bright.

With every sigh, a new journey begins,
Chasing the echoes of life in the spins.
Moonbeams awaken the stories untold,
Embracing the warmth as the night turns bold.

In twilight's embrace, we uncover the truth,
Each moment a treasure reclaimed from our youth.
The softness surrounds, a comforting shroud,
Wrapped in its whispers, we rise, unbowed.

As time gently lapses, the night takes the stage,
With dreams long forgotten, we turn a new page.
Cradled in starlight, lost stories replay,
In twilight's embrace, forever we stay.

www.ingramcontent.com/pod-product-compliance
Ingram Content Group UK Ltd.
Pitfield, Milton Keynes, MK11 3LW, UK
UKHW031956131224
452403UK00010B/524